P9-DYB-167

The
MAD
TELL IT LIKE IT IS
Book

Written By
LOU SILVERSTONE

Illustrated By
BOB JONES

Edited by
Nick Meglin

WARNER BOOKS

A Warner Communications Company

CONTENTS

Senator Redneck, just what is the aim of the **new right?**
We want to return to those glorious days of yesteryear when this country was **great!** When **ladies** wore dresses! Real men wore **crewcuts!** An' instead of watchin' sex and violence on TV, we lissened to the darkies singin' good old American songs like, **"Ol' Black Joe"!** They shore don't write them like **that** anymore!

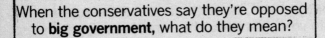

What important legislation are you planning to introduce in the Senate?
I'm presenting the most **important bill** since the Bill of Rights—the **Family Prayer in School and Dancin'** Law! It will make school prayer mandatory, strengthen the family, and make the Square Dance ouah National Folk Dance!

Could you give us some details on how your bill will strengthen the family?
It will give parents the right to censor text books! It will forbid sex education in the schools, ban mixin' of the sexes at school functions! And most important of all, parents will have the right to punish their children as they see fit—without them bleedin' heart liberals cryin "child abuse!" Like Ah always say, "Spare the rod and spoil the fun!"
WHAP

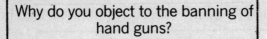

One last question—you've been quoted as saying you want the government off the backs of the people! Yet, you're asking for laws that will allow the government to violate **everybody's** privacy!
CLICK
CLICK
Right! Ah want the guvment off ouah backs and into more **interestin'** places—like the school room, the church, the libraries, the doctor's office, the theater, living rooms and **especially,** the **bedrooms!** Hoo Boy!

WE BREAK FOR
COMMERCIALS I

I'm the Buyer Aspirin Man and I want you to know Buyer's is the best pain reliever that money can buy!

A TELL IT LIKE IT IS

DOUBLE FEATURE

"The CHAMPIONSHIP BELT"
a Boxing Flick à la Hollywood

WE BREAK FOR
COMMERCIALS II

FEATURE II

"The CHAMPIONSHIP GELT"
a Boxing Flick à la
Real Life

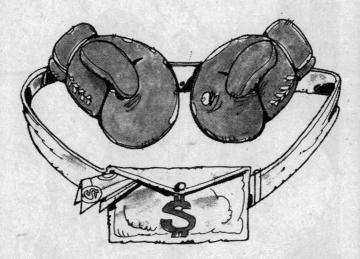

I'm prepared to offer your man a shot at the heavyweight championship of the world...
We might consider it for a **five million guarantee** in addition to 50% of all ancillary rights, including closed-circuit TV, T-shirts, programs, refreshments plus a percentage of electronic games and "Kid" dolls.

Boxing history is being written here tonight in Las Vegas! In all my years of broadcasting championship fights, never have I seen so many **celebrities!** There's Frank and Don and Sammy; Sylvester, Barbra, Dolly, The President and The First Lady…
KID VS CHAMP

My **lawyer** is responsible for my winning! He put the **return bout** clause in the contract! That means The Champ would let **me** win this time, then **he'd** try to regain the title in the **return bout** on home TV! The gullible public will demand a **third** match which will be on **closed circuit!** Instead of having **one** big payday, we get **three!**
This is Howard Coolsell telling it like it is from Las Vegas...

WE BREAK FOR COMMERCIALS III

Is your pet tired of the same old, dull dog food?

CHOW WAGON TO THE RESCUE!!!

Sure he ate the **horses!** What do you think most dog food is **made** from?

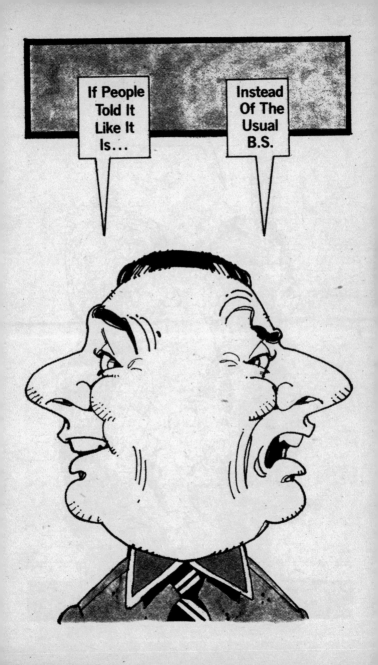

B.S.:

B.S.:

Like It Is:

B.S.:

B.S.:

Every summer desperate parents get rid of their kids by shipping them off to camp so they can get the benefit of green grass, fresh air, blue skies and like that! That's okay for *city kids* who never get to see that kind of stuff! But how about the *suburban kids* who are surrounded all year by boring Mother Nature! We think there should be a camp for *them* with a *different* environment! A place in the Big Apple like...

"A unique experience for
the suburban child."

The teen years are important to your child's development. It's a time when a youth should be expanding horizons and facing new challenges. At Citi-Glumi your children will face the greatest challenge of all—survival!

There are no green slopes, sparkling lakes, blue skies, cool woodland, or fresh air at Citi-Glumi. Your child will spend the summer in an entirely new environment! The camp is located in the core of the Big Apple, or, as our campers like to describe it, "The Pits!" While Citi-Glumi is a non-sectarian camp, we find that after attending just one summer, many children have turned to religion. This usually happens during our over-night camp-out trip. As a wise man once said, "There are no atheists in Central Park after dark—or in the daytime for that matter!"

Our highly trained counselors.

Even though our camp is designed to meet the needs of the suburban child, many big city liberal families will find Citi-Glumi an ideal place for their children to spend the summer. They will discover a new city, a city they thought existed only on TV or in the movies! A city away from the sheltered private school and housekeeper atmosphere! Here they will meet real, live minority children and share a meaningful camping experience they will never forget, even with psychiatric help!

Learning to swim at City-Glumi.

ARTS & CRAFTS

SPRAY PAINTING Our campers don't spend their time making silly ashtrays or leather wallets! No, the City-Glumi camper is allowed to express himself with a stimulating creative experience–spray painting. The sight of his name in brightly colored, 4 foot letters on a subway car–knowing his handiwork will be seen by millions of subway riders–gives your child a sense of accomplishment and achievement he's never had before, and is particularly helpful to the youngster with an identity problem!

Let us spray…

WOODCARVING This activity is recommended for the older camper. Armed with a standard city switch blade knife, he gets to carve up restaurant tables, park benches, plastic subway seats, or wherever he feels the creative urge. Does it end at City-Glumi? Not on your life—watch what he does to the furniture when he gets home!

Campers carving out a niche for themselves.

SOCIAL ACTIVITIES

CAMP FIRE Most camps offer the same boring nightime get-together–sitting around the campfire, roasting marshmallows, and singing square songs like "One Can of Beer on the Wall." But at Citi-Glumi your child will witness a real fire in an abandoned (Usually) tenement, torched by an arsonist! It is a rewarding experience for the camper, watching the firemen desperately battling to control the blaze while being pelted with debris by people in the neighborhood.

Memorable nights around the campfire.

ADVENTURE

NATURE WALKS You can forget about poison ivy on our nature walks! Our pot-holed trails wind through wonderful areas to observe close-up city wildlife in its most natural and unnatural state. Who could not marvel at the gigantic rodents living among the festering piles of garbage, or at earth's oldest creature–the cockroach–in unbelievable numbers? Not to mention the wide variety of strange creatures indigenous to the Times Square, Bowery, and Greenwich Village areas.

It's only human nature.

ARCHAELOGICAL TRIPS Explore the ruins of South Bronx, the roads of Staten Island, the schools of Brooklyn, and the snow-removal equipment of Queens.

Something old, nothing new.

Talk about gut reaction!

FIELD STUDY This series of trips was organized for the curious of mind and strong of stomach! Exciting new challenges await those who dare confront such famous landmarks as Manhattan's East Side Doggy-doo Swamp and Coney Island Beaches.

DEATH RIDE A trip on the subway might very well be the highlight of the summer's adventure program. The camper boards the crowded, filthy subway car and as the door slams closed on someone's foot, he's off on the ride of his life! Above the deafening roar of his seemingly square-wheeled vehicle, he'll hear the curses of fellow passengers or perhaps the screams of terrified victims as teenage hoodlums mug and molest in their inimitable way. Who knows—with any kind of luck he can be a victim himself! The camper will experience the thrill of being stuck between stations in an over-heated, darkened car, never knowing when—or if—he'll be rescued!

Going along for the ride.

SPORTS

TEAM SPORTS It doesn't matter whether you win or lose or how you play the game! The only thing that matters is whether you survive! With this motto in mind, Citi-Glumi conducts a sports program designed for developing a healthy body, with particular emphasis on running fast, since this ability will often determine whether or not the body will live long enough to become healthy. This is achieved through competitive games like "Rumble." Here, teams face-off and attempt to defend their "turf." The team with the fewest casualties is proclaimed "winner."

Teams lining up for a game of rumble.

SWIMMING Citi-Glumi has several rotting piers from which campers can dive into the fabulous Hudson River with its distinct ooze, oil slick, and floating debris. And while such conditions make water skiing impossible, it does create the opportunity for trying out the new fun craze, "walking on water."

Fun at the ol' swimming hole.

WATER SPORTS FOR NON-SWIMMERS A rusty, old fire hydrant provides the camper with a steady stream of water that serves to cool off his buddies as well as drench passing cars. It's all part of the summer fun at Citi-Glumi!

Let us spray.

MEALS

Forget about the tiresome camp fare served in boring mess halls! Every meal at City-Glumi is a culinary experience! The campers gorge themselves on international menus at famous fast food restaurants. The specialties include slimy pizza, greasy hot dogs, yecchy burgers, soggy custard—washed down with watered orange drink. One summer at City-Glumi and your child will be a lot more appreciative of your home cooking!

Chow time is wow time!

ACCOMMODATIONS

Sleeping quarters are located in authentic, colorful tenements. Every floor has its own toilet and some of them actually work. At night, the camper and his 17 bunkmates are lulled to sleep by the screaming fire engines and police cars, the roar of the subway, the blaring of over-sized portables bellowing disco, and the cries of "Help!" from local crime victims. The camper also learns the technique of sleeping with one eye open to avoid being ripped off of watches, wallets, contact lenses, or pajamas by his buddies. And in the morning, it is no bugle that signals the start of another adventure-filled day at Citi-Glumi, it is the sound of banging garbage cans as sanitation workers announce their appointed rounds.

Typical bunk at Citi-Glumi.

Camp City-Glumi

WE BREAK FOR COMMERCIALS IV

VISIT to a ROADSIDE FRUIT STAND

WE BREAK FOR
COMMERCIALS V

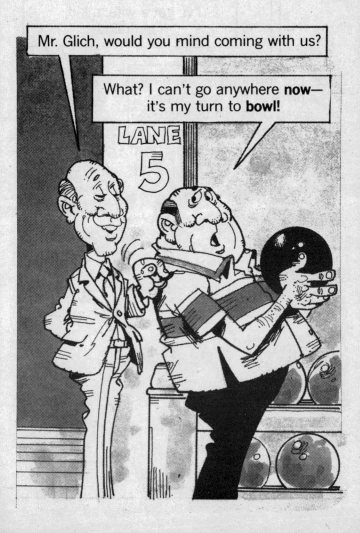

WE SEE TOO MANY TV SHOWS THAT AD-DRESS THEMSELVES TO VARIOUS ASPECTS OF THE JUDICIAL SYSTEM! WE SEE TOO FEW TV SHOWS THAT ADDRESS THEMSELVES TO THESE VARIOUS ASPECTS WITH THE

TELL-IT-LIKE-IT-IS

APPROACH! WE NOW PRESENT A TRILOGY OF

TV SHOWS

THAT WILL CHANGE ALL THAT! STAY TUNED FOR...

THE

THE

STOOLIE

Dames, you can't reason wit' 'em! I was late—the Chief was already at my office! I hated him beatin' me there—he takes all the dimes!

Somebody's tipping off the mob on when and where we're gonna make a raid! When we get there the perpetrators have already split! I want **you** to find out who the lousy fink is, uh, no offense meant...
None taken, Chief! Finque's the name, and fink's my game!

I headed for the *Grape Vine*, a watering hole where the mob guys hung out! I ordered a beer and listened! There was the usual gossip one hears at a bar…

My patience finally paid off…

Hi, Dick Caveat again! Remember when the U.S.A. was the good guy and never lost a war? That was when psychologists had nothing to do with the armed forces, except ask recruits if they liked girls! But times have changed and today the psychologist is a **key member** of the military team! To find out about the new role they play in warfare, we're going to interview Dr. Sigmund Lobotomy, who has been chosen as the...

"TELL-IT-LIKE-IT-IS" MILITARY PSYCHOLOGIST of the YEAR

Doctor, why have psychologists become so important in modern warfare?
In a word, progress! War used to be a simple exercise. Soldiers would shoot at each other and whichever army killed the most, won! Today, thanks to psychological methodology, war is complicated! Men have to be taught behavioral patterns, are programmed, tested and then they shoot each other and whichever army kills the most, wins.
That's progress?

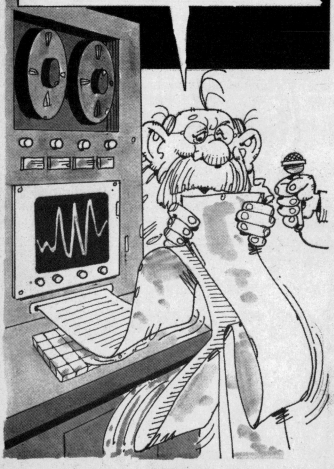

WE BREAK FOR
COMMERCIALS VII

Since fairy tales were written hundreds of years ago, they don't make much sense today! So we decided to update them! Naturally, they <u>still</u> don't make much sense!

TELL IT
LIKE IT IS

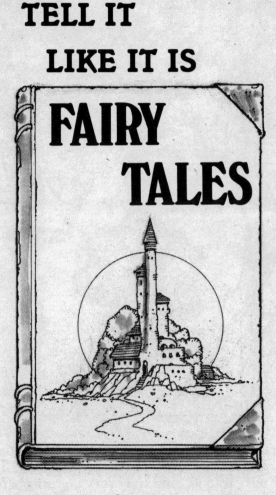

FAIRY
TALES

Once upon a time there were three bears, a papa bear, a mama bear and a little baby bear. The bears were into jogging and every morning before breakfast they would jog in the forest.

One day a little girl named Goldilocks was walking in the forest when she came upon the house
where the three bears lived. She knocked on the
door but there was no answer. The bears were out
jogging. Goldilocks went into the house. Her
mother had warned her never to go into strange
cars but hadn't mentioned strange cottages in
the forest.

Goldilocks went into the living room. She saw three chairs, a big chair for the papa bear, a medium-sized chair for the mama bear and a small chair for the baby bear. But there was something missing. There was no TV set! So Goldilocks didn't bother sitting in any of the chairs. What's the sense of sitting in the living room if you can't watch TV, right?

Next Goldilocks went into the kitchen. There were three bowls on the table. Goldilocks tasted the food in the bowls.

Goldilocks looked in the cupboard to see if she could find some **decent** food, like Sugar Puffs, Cocoa Sucrose, or potato chips! But all she found was more porridge! Yeecchh!

Goldilocks left the house in the forest and never went back.

Once upon a time there were 3 little pigs. Each one decided to build a house for himself.

But the first pig didn't listen and built a house out of straw. The big bad wolf came along, huffed and puffed and blew the house down and he ate the pig.

Hey, did you hear what happened to our brother the shmuck in the straw house?

Yeah, but **I'm** not worried! I'm building my house out of **wood!**

Wood's no good! It will warp in the rain, and you'll get termites—not to mention a huffing, puffing wolf!

The second pig built his house out of wood, the big bad wolf came along, did his huffing thing, blew the house down and ate the pig. The third pig decided to build his house out of *brick!*

And so the third little pig built a house out of simulated brick siding. Along came the wolf, he huffed and he puffed…

...and he blew the house down! Naturally, he ate the third little pig! But wait—the wolf had been such a hog (you should pardon the pun), that he had eaten the 3 pigs without bothering to *cook* them! He got a *trichinosis infestation* from eating uncooked pork and lived *miserably* ever after!

Once upon a time there was a boy named Jack. He lived with his mother and they were very poor. In fact, they didn't have enough to eat. Their only possession was a cow. Jack's mother decided to sell the cow so they could get some money for food.

On his way to the market, Jack met a man who asked him where he was going...

Jack traded the cow for the beans but he had a feeling his mother wasn't going to be thrilled since beans gave her *gas!*

Jack's mother was right—the government paid them for not growing beans and they lived happily ever after on government subsidies!

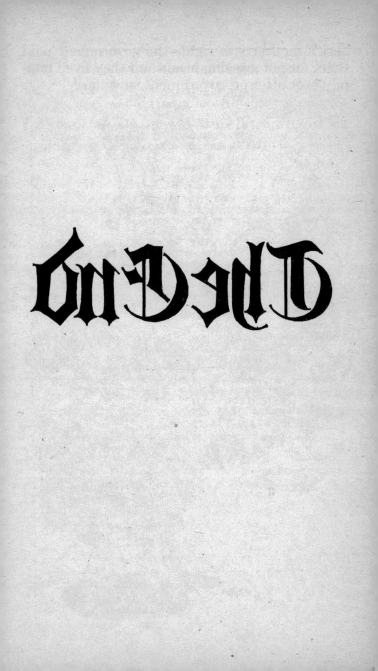

The End